Online News

Martin Gitlin

Published in the United States of America by Cherry Lake Publishing
Ann Arbor, Michigan
www.cherrylakepublishing.com

Reading Adviser: Marla Conn, MS, Ed., Literacy specialist, Read-Ability, Inc.

Photo Credits: ©sebra/Shutterstock.com, cover; ©Csondy/iStock, 5; ©Everett Collection/Shutterstock.com, 6; ©O'Halloran, Thomas J., photographer/Library of Congress/Reproduction No. LC-DIG-ppmsca-03134, 7; ©Dusan Petkovic/Shutterstock.com, 8; ©1000 Words/Shutterstock.com, 11; ©ultramansk/Shutterstock.com, 12; ©Rawpixel.com/Shutterstock.com, 13; ©roundex/Shutterstock.com, 14; ©duangphorn wiriya/Shutterstock.com, 17; © Microgen/Shutterstock.com, 18; ©Ian Warren/Shutterstock.com, 20; ©J. Ottmann Lith. Co./Library of Congress/Reproduction No. LC-DIG-ppmsca-25569, 23; ©Sonia Bonet/Shutterstock.com, 24; ©bangoland/Shutterstock.com, 26

Graphic Element Credits: ©Ohn Mar/Shutterstock.com, back cover, multiple interior pages; ©Dmitrieva Katerina/Shutterstock.com, back cover, multiple interior pages; ©advent/Shutterstock.com, back cover, front cover, multiple interior pages; ©Visual Generation/Shutterstock.com, multiple interior pages; ©anfisa focusova/Shutterstock.com, front cover, multiple interior pages; ©Babich Alexander/Shutterstock.com, back cover, front cover, multiple interior pages

Library of Congress Cataloging-in-Publication Data has been filed and is available at catalog.loc.gov

Printed in the United States of America
Corporate Graphics

Martin Gitlin has written more than 150 educational books. He also won more than 45 awards during his 11-year career as a newspaper journalist. Gitlin lives in Cleveland, Ohio.

Table of Contents

CHAPTER ONE

Extra! Extra!

It could have been anytime between the 1950s and 1980s. A familiar sound was heard every morning in most American homes. It was the sound of the newspaper landing on the front porch. Families were eager to read it. The kids scrambled to get to the comics first. Parents would read about the news, from local to around the globe. For a long time, this was the fastest way of staying informed about the world.

There was no cable TV. There were no personal computers. There was no internet. There were no smartphones. There was no social media like Facebook and Twitter. There was no 24-hour news cycle.

The peak of the traditional newspaper industry was in 1990.

The radio became a news medium during the 1920s. After World War II, it became an important source for breaking news.

How People Stayed Informed: Then

People used to stay informed by reading, listening to, and watching the news. They read the newspaper in the morning. They listened to the radio to and from their way to work or school. They watched the news on TV. But back then, television only had a few channels. It wasn't until cable began in the late 1940s that more channels appeared.

The famous *The New York Times* and *The Washington Post* have received a lot of free publicity from President Donald Trump. Trump has criticized both papers for what he claims to be negative coverage of his job performance. Trump has claimed that they publish "fake news."

By the early 1960s, surveys indicated that people preferred watching the news on television.

About 36 percent of young adults ages 18 to 29 confirm that social media is their primary source for news. This number is 14 percent in people ages 50 to 64.

How People Stay Informed: Now

Times have changed. People can **download apps** that provide news anytime, anywhere. They can click on hundreds of news sites on their laptops, smartphones, or iPads. People today have access to thousands of these news sources that deliver different viewpoints in different ways— from serious BuzzFeed articles interjected with non-serious GIFs and memes to 280-character tweets to Facebook posts. Some feel that certain news sources are **biased** and provide more opinions than facts.

Social media has forever changed the world of news. News can now be delivered and received instantly. People can find news from far more sources than ever before. Anyone with an opinion can shout it out to the world. But whether these changes are positive is up for debate.

A New World for Newspapers

There has been nothing but bad news for newspapers' print editions in recent years. The **circulation** of American papers dropped to a 77-year low in 2017. Six million fewer people read newspapers that year than they did in 1940. And money from advertising fell by more than half from 2005 to 2014 alone.

Those are disturbing statistics given that the American population has grown by more than 190 million since 1940. But not all the news is bad for newspapers. Millions of Americans are clicking on their online sites. The most popular print newspapers are also the most popular **digital** papers. *The New York Times* boasts one of the most downloaded news apps in the country.

It costs news consumers money to read some major newspapers online. But that has not stopped millions of Americans from checking out what they report about politics and other issues.

CHAPTER TWO

Our Changing Sources

The news about news was no surprise. A survey in 2018 revealed that fewer Americans than ever were reading the paper. Social media passed print newspapers as a preferred news source for the first time. About 1 in 5 Americans stated that they often use such sites as Facebook or Twitter. Only 1 in 6 said the same about newspapers.

That was not the only bad news for newspapers. The survey showed that the future looked even bleaker. More than 1 in 3 people under age 30 use social media as their primary news source. Only 2 out of every 100 people that age consider print newspapers their first choice. The trend among youth toward social media and away from newspapers seems here to stay.

Television news is more popular with people 65 years and older. About 81 percent primarily get their news from TV, whereas only 16 percent of people ages 18 to 29 do.

It's Not All Downhill for Traditional News

According to the same survey, television remains the top news source in the United States. Nearly half of all Americans still turn on the TV for their news and one-third click on TV news websites. However, some of these news sources have been criticized for biased reporting. Fox News promotes **conservative** social and political views. **Liberal** network MSNBC does not hide its agenda either. News reports on networks such as NBC, ABC, and CBS are viewed by most as neutral. But television is certainly not the wave of the future. Only about 1 in 6 Americans under age 30 regularly watches TV news.

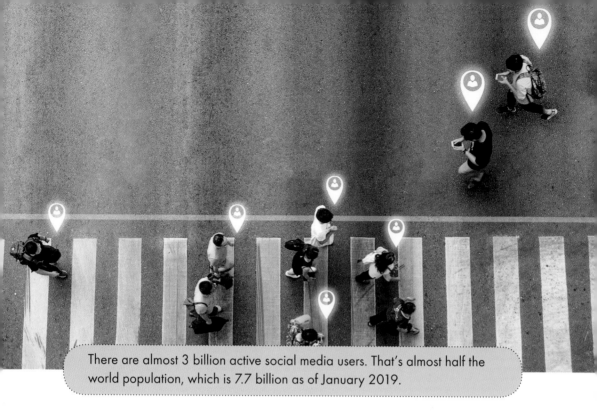

There are almost 3 billion active social media users. That's almost half the world population, which is 7.7 billion as of January 2019.

Social Media

Some consider the trend toward social media news alarming. Many people who post or link articles on Facebook and Twitter are not unbiased. More often than not, these articles are opinion-based or only present information and facts that agree with the argument being made. A recent report revealed that the number of Americans who use social media for

Facebook is among the most popular sites on the internet. But it found trouble when it was revealed that Russians secretly placed ads on the site during the 2016 U.S. presidential campaign. The ads were placed to promote Donald Trump and **dissuade** readers from voting for Hillary Clinton.

Facebook, YouTube, Twitter, and Reddit are the top social media platforms that people check for the latest news.

About 70 percent of news journalists believe that Twitter is a valuable resource and network for sharing the news.

news doubled from 2013 to 2016 alone. It also indicated that more 18- to 24-year-olds preferred social media over television as a news source.

The good news is that people are aware of the inaccuracies social media news can present. According to a survey, about 57 percent of Americans who get their news on social media don't believe everything they read.

This makes social media sites very important to the future of the country. These sites and their users should work toward providing accurate news based on facts and not on feelings or opinions.

We Just Want the Truth

Many social media and news website readers know biased reporting when they see it. But for others, it is hard to judge. Who doesn't like to click on sites that offer the same views as their own?

Most consumers want their news straight. They then form their own opinions based on true information. But they do not always know where to find it. They would like to know which sources provide the most unbiased news.

Some online sites, like AllSides, provide ratings. AllSides ranks online news sources and provides information on whether these sources lean liberal or conservative.

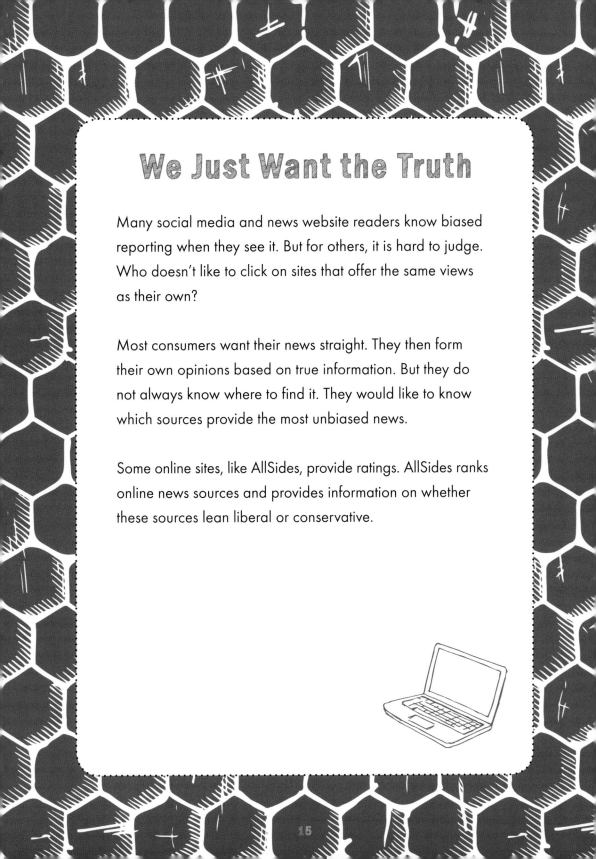

CHAPTER THREE

Good News, Bad News

The Mary Tyler Moore Show was a popular television sitcom in the 1970s. The legendary program about a TV newsroom featured a boss named Lou Grant. In one episode, he was arguing against changing the format of his news program. And he uttered three words that are still relevant: "News is truth."

What is packaged as news today is often not truth. It's opinion packaged to look like the truth. That is especially true on social media, though more than half of social media users know this.

Some online news sites and social media platforms are more popular with one gender than the other. For example, Reddit is more than twice as popular among men. LinkedIn is also used far more by men. Women tend to gravitate toward Facebook and Snapchat for their news.

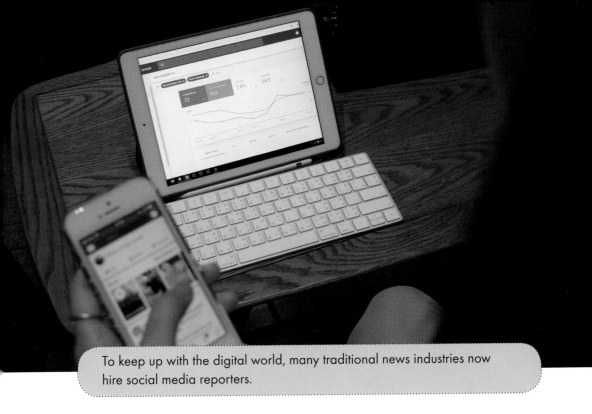

To keep up with the digital world, many traditional news industries now hire social media reporters.

The Good News

News on social media isn't all bad. In fact, about 36 percent of people who check social media for the news believe platforms like Twitter and Facebook have helped them understand current events. People also like that the news is easily accessible. In fact, about 21 percent of social media users say this. It's convenient to just search their Twitter or Facebook feed for the news. And about 8 percent claim they enjoy the social interaction— they like discussing the news with people from all over.

Journalists use social media to gather information, share published news stories, and interact with the users.

Many Options

The number of social media and online news options has grown. But there is no doubt about which is most popular. A 2018 poll conducted by the Pew Research Center revealed that nearly half of American adults use Facebook to become informed. Other popular sites and platforms include YouTube, Twitter, Instagram, LinkedIn, Reddit, and Snapchat.

The wave of the future? Many claim that social platforms, like Snapchat and Instagram, are the wave of the future when it comes to news. A study showed that about 3 in 4 Americans ages 18 to 29 use Snapchat to get their news. More than half check Instagram.

News: Social Media vs. Other Media

Study after study reveals that the majority of people know that news on social media is biased. So why is it still more popular as a news source than local or national TV news or reputable online newspapers? Experts say it is because of convenience. It's a lot easier to check the news on one platform from a variety of sources at the same time.

The invention of the smartphone popularized social media and gave rise to citizen journalism.

Gen Z

The younger generation may also be a big reason why social media is becoming the number one go-to for the news. According to a study, **Gen Z** social media users rely on Twitter for breaking news. In the United States, there are about 86 million Gen Zers as of 2017. That's a lot of people heading to Twitter for the news! The majority of this generation believes that Twitter provides the best real-time news from actual real people. This is commonly called "citizen journalism." They prefer the live video streams and the real-time tweets from real people in the middle of the action. Gen Z believes this type of news is more authentic than news provided by anchors or journalists from a news agency.

The Buzz About BuzzFeed

One unique online news website is BuzzFeed. It has gone through a radical change—for good reasons. One reason is an American Trends Panel poll that asked readers to rank their trust level of 36 online news sources. BuzzFeed placed close to dead last, despite having won **journalism** awards.

The problem was its format. BuzzFeed created what became known as listicles. They were articles in the form of lists. The site also published quizzes and other material that did not fall under the category of news. That format was fun to read, but it did not bring trust as a legitimate news source. BuzzFeed has worked to change that. It placed all of its news articles on a separate website called BuzzFeed News. Gone are the "listicles," and in their place are more traditional news articles.

MarketWatch cites one problem with this news site, which was launched in 2018. The claim is that BuzzFeed does not provide straight news. MarketWatch lists BuzzFeed News articles as being fairly biased.

CHAPTER FOUR

Informed or Confused?

The term *fake news* can be traced all the way back to the 1890s. But it has been made famous in the modern era. *Collins Dictionary* even gave *fake news* its Word of the Year honors in 2017. What is fake news? It is basically lying by media outlets seeking to sway people toward their side of an issue. Fake news has exploded in the era of social media.

Americans seeking truth and easy access to news have found that getting both is nearly impossible. Many people download social media apps such as Facebook, Twitter, and Snapchat to their smartphones. Online news sources fight for the attention of those social media sites so they can get reposted, retweeted, or published directly onto those platforms.

Fake news isn't new. Before social media, it used to be referred to as propaganda or yellow journalism.

THE "REDS" AND THE "YELLOWS."

Journalists try their best to tell accurate, unbiased news, both on and off social media.

Where's the Truth?

People given so many options can easily get confused. Which sources offer biased or opinion-based news? Which offer fact-based news? Nearly every American adult admits confusion by fake news. Age does not matter. Level of education does not matter. Race does not matter. Political leaning does not matter. A 2018 Pew Research poll revealed that nearly all Americans believe that fake news makes it hard to find the truth.

Getting Techie with the News

Meanwhile, the battle rages on social media and the internet to attract news consumers. The Discover App offered by Snapchat features news sites such as BuzzFeed and *The Wall Street Journal*. Facebook created its Instant Articles app for many publishers, including news sites like the *The Wall Street Journal*. Google launched Google News. Twitter followed with an app called Moments, which features a variety of trending news.

Most apps and online news websites feature comment sections. They are often filled with thousands of reactions from readers expressing opinions on news stories. The internet and social media allow people to stage heated arguments without seeing a face or hearing a voice. They can argue without knowing the person they disagree with. Many believe this allows people to be meaner.

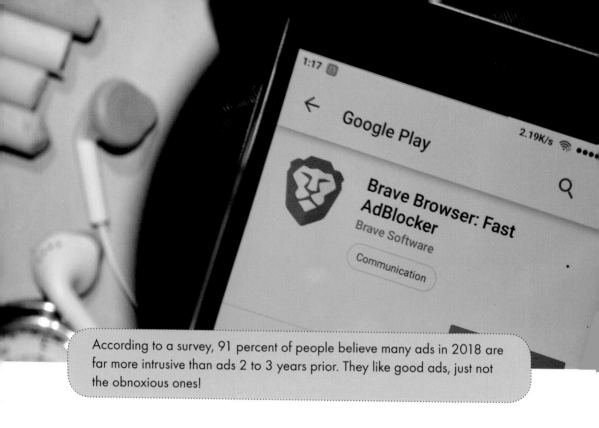

According to a survey, 91 percent of people believe many ads in 2018 are far more intrusive than ads 2 to 3 years prior. They like good ads, just not the obnoxious ones!

Each company has tried to get an edge on the competition. Among them is Apple, which announced it would allow ad-blocking **software** to be downloaded from its app store. Online readers prefer to get their news without seeing ads on the page. They are like television viewers who fast-forward through commercials.

How will that affect publishers who depend on advertising to make money? Will companies spend big bucks to run ads on social media and websites in which those ads can be blocked? These are questions that will be answered in the future. What will the future of news look like? Nobody knows for sure. What is certain is that social media and new **technology** will play a huge role.

Best of the Best

The modern era of social media has made one thing clear. People do not only want to read the news. They are not content just to be informed. They yearn to voice their opinions on what is happening around the world.

That is why the most popular news apps are those that encourage participation. A ranking of apps in the United States revealed that the top two news apps are Twitter and Reddit. Both allow readers to react to the news of the day and express their views. Nearly 70 million Americans have Twitter accounts. More than 300 million are active users worldwide.

Timeline

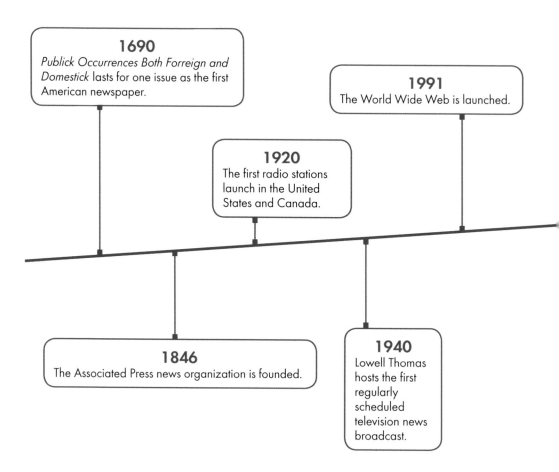

1690
Publick Occurrences Both Forreign and Domestick lasts for one issue as the first American newspaper.

1991
The World Wide Web is launched.

1920
The first radio stations launch in the United States and Canada.

1846
The Associated Press news organization is founded.

1940
Lowell Thomas hosts the first regularly scheduled television news broadcast.

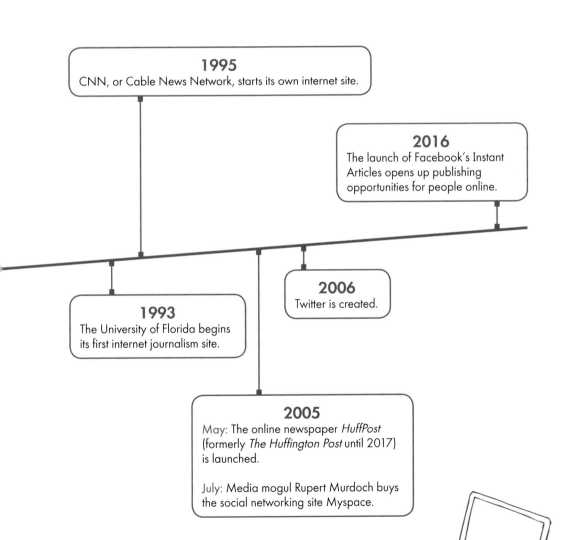

1995
CNN, or Cable News Network, starts its own internet site.

2016
The launch of Facebook's Instant Articles opens up publishing opportunities for people online.

1993
The University of Florida begins its first internet journalism site.

2006
Twitter is created.

2005
May: The online newspaper *HuffPost* (formerly *The Huffington Post* until 2017) is launched.

July: Media mogul Rupert Murdoch buys the social networking site Myspace.

Learn More

Books
Dell, Pamela. *Understanding the News.* North Mankato, MN: Capstone Press, 2018.

Rowell, Rebecca. *Social Media: Like It or Leave It.* North Mankato, MN: Compass Point Books, 2015.

Websites
Time for Kids
https://www.timeforkids.com
One of the most respected news magazines invites kids to learn about the news.

DOGO News
https://www.dogonews.com
This site features fun articles about current events and more.

Glossary

apps (APS) applications downloaded to a mobile device

biased (BYE-uhsd) favoring one way of thinking over another

circulation (sur-kyuh-LAY-shuhn) number of copies sold, such as of a newspaper

conservative (kuhn-SUR-vuh-tiv) tending to agree with traditional views or values

digital (DIJ-ih-tuhl) related to computer technology

dissuade (dis-WAYD) to convince someone not to do something

download (DOUN-lohd) to transfer data from a larger computer to a smaller device

Gen Z (JEN ZEE) people born in the mid-1990s to early 2000s

journalism (JUR-nuh-liz-uhm) the collecting and editing of news

liberal (LIB-ur-uhl) not tied to traditional beliefs

software (SAWFT-wair) programs and related information used by a computer

technology (tek-NAH-luh-jee) use of science to solve problems

Index